BITTER TART

MILANO
HANDCRAFTED FROM AGAVE AZUL

BITTER TART

60 SHARP AND SOUR COCKTAILS TO TICKLE YOUR TASTEBUDS

CONTENTS

TART COCKTAILS 112

MEXICO
TEQUILA
VERMOUTH
ROSSO
1863

INTRODUCTION

Bitter Tart is not just a collection of cocktail recipes, but an invitation to reclaim your evening. This is about the joy of discovering new flavours, experimenting with old favourites, and treating yourself to something a little special – whether you're celebrating with friends or the simple pleasure of a cosy night in with a loved one after a long week.

We know what you're thinking: why bitter and tart? Well, let's face it – life's too short for dull drinks, and nothing cuts through the noise quite like the sharp tang of a well-made cocktail. Bitter and tart flavours have a unique way of waking up your palate, making every sip feel like a mini adventure. In our opinion, they're the heroes of the cocktail world and we're here to make sure they get the spotlight they deserve.

We're here to show you that with a few key pieces of equipment, a handful of ingredients, and a little know-how, you can turn your home into your very own speakeasy. And trust us, once you've got the basics down, you'll never look back.

The Bitter and the Tart

As you flip through these pages, you'll find the recipes are split into two distinct categories: bitter and tart. The bitter cocktails are bracing, bold, and a little rebellious – perfect for those moments when you need a drink that says, "I'm here to be noticed." Whether it's a classic Negroni or an edgier Campari Spritz, these drinks are unapologetically strong and complex, just like you after a few sips.

On the flip side, the tart cocktails are zesty, refreshing, and full of attitude. From a perfectly chilled Daiquiri to a zingy Cosmopolitan, these drinks are here to remind you that sometimes, life's better with a little extra pucker. Tart cocktails are for when you want to feel alive – whether that's after a long day, before a big night out or during a sun-soaked afternoon on the balcony.

Tools of the Trade

Before we dive into the recipes, let's talk equipment. No, you don't need a fancy bar cart or a degree in mixology to make great cocktails, but there are a few essentials that will make your life a lot easier – and your drinks a lot tastier. Think of these tools as your cocktail arsenal, ready to help you stir, shake, and garnish your way to greatness.

We'll guide you through everything you need, from glassware and shakers to the trusty jigger and cocktail strainer. And don't worry, if you're the type who likes to go the extra mile (or just look extra stylish), we've also got tips on how to stock your bar like a pro. After all, what's the point of a good cocktail if you can't show it off in a chic glass?

Mastering Techniques

Of course, great cocktails are about more than just following a recipe – they're about technique. Whether you're shaking up a citrusy concoction or stirring a spirit-forward classic, knowing when to shake and when to stir can make all the difference. We'll walk you through the basics of cocktail making, from muddling and straining to creating perfect ice (trust us, it matters). We'll even let you in on the secret of mastering bitters and citrus, two essential elements that can take any drink from good to absolutely unforgettable.

Bitter But Not Heartless

Whether you're revelling in the bliss of a quiet night in with friends or you've found yourself with a moment spare amid the chaos of everyday life, the cocktails in this book are the perfect accompaniment. So switch off your phone, grab your shaker and your favourite glasses and let's toast to the perfect balance of bitter and tart. Because life is too short for boring drinks, and you, your friends, and love interests deserve a cocktail that's as bold and vibrant as you are.

Cheers to the good times – with great drinks!

THE BASICS

EQUIPMENT

You can make drinks with virtually no bar equipment, but it's difficult to make great drinks with little more than the basics. You don't need to transform your living room into a proper bar, but if you want to make a good impression then it's worth investing in the essentials: a shaker, for example, the right glasses, a good range of spirits, liqueurs and bitters. You'll want to know how to open a bottle of champagne and how to cut a twist. In time you'll realize that what turns an ordinary drink into a work of art is simply attention to detail: using orange or Peychaud's bitters instead of Angostura, even just knowing how important good-quality ice is. Small and inexpensive touches that make all the difference.

Cocktail Shakers

Shakers come in a mass of shapes and sizes and while it might seem like a good idea to invest in a novelty one, run three simple checks before you part with your money. Firstly, is it easy to hold? It's pointless having a baroque instrument on the bar if you drop it all the time. Secondly, is it easy to use? Does the lid get stuck, or fall off, and can you strain easily? Thirdly, is it made from stainless steel or glass? If it isn't, don't buy it.

Many bartenders use a Boston shaker. This comes in two parts: one a tall thick glass, the other similarly shaped but slightly smaller and made of stainless steel. This part fits inside the top of the glass part, allowing you to shake the ice and liquid between the two. You can also use the glass part for stirring drinks and, because it's clear, it allows you to see if your proportions are correct. Be warned, Boston shakers can be tricky to separate.

Juggling

You may, in time, decide to try and copy that hotshot barkeep you saw working the crowd in Las Vegas with his juggling tricks. Our advice is DON'T. Flair bartending – as juggling bottles, glasses and shakers is known – is great fun to watch but, without wishing to be too much of a killjoy, the most important element in preparing a drink is making sure the drink is made correctly and tastes good. Anyway, it can make a dreadful mess of the carpet.

GLASSES

Shot

It's fairly obvious what this glass is for. Small shots of the hard stuff intended to be drunk quickly – frozen vodka, tequila, etc. They can double up as measures if needed.

Old-Fashioned

Great for the eponymous cocktail (or variants thereof) which can be built in the glass, or for old-fashioned drinks like whisky and soda.

Collins (Tall)

The shape shows that this is a glass intended for long drinks, not just members of the Collins family but a Gin and Tonic is perfect in this, as are Mojitos and Mint Juleps.

Champagne flute

The perfect shape to encourage a regular, prolonged stream of bubbles – different from the classic coupe which doesn't preserve the fizz for as long.

Wine glass

Red wines and great whites need to breathe in the glass to release their aroma. A wide-mouthed goblet not only does this but also allows you to swirl the wine to see the colour.

Champagne saucer

Use this for any short mixed drink: Daiquiri, Sours, etc.

Highball

Use this for making long drinks, modern, fruity cocktails, Bloody Mary, etc.

Martini (Cocktail)

The classic shape for all short mixed drinks, such as Martini and Manhattan. Three rules:

- make sure the glasses are cold;
- hold them by the stem while drinking (or the drink will heat up);
- buy smaller rather than larger examples.

BAR ACCESSORIES

Mixing glass

This is an essential piece of kit you can't be without.

Measure/Jigger

Use a measure until you feel confident to measure by eye.

Measuring spoons

To gauge those vital small additions.

Ice bucket

Keep it full.

Ice scoop

To ladle in the ice when making frozen drinks.

Straws

These come in different lengths and widths, depending on the type of drink being served. They are necessary for longer drinks.

Chopping board

Use as a preparation surface when making drinks, chopping up fruit, herbs and other garnishes.

Sharp knife

Especially important for preparing garnishes.

Cocktail sticks

Handy for securing olives, onions, cherries and other fruit.

Swizzle sticks

Useful for stirring long drinks.

Ice tongs

Use tongs instead of your hands to pick up ice, otherwise it will melt.

Strainer

To ensure that no bits of ice end up in the drink.

BARTENDING CHECKLIST

Alcohol

- Gin (kept in fridge or freezer)
- Sloe gin
- Vodka (kept in fridge or freezer)
- Flavoured vodka
- White rum
- Gold/dark rum
- Tequila (100 per cent blue agave silver/reposado)
- Bourbon
- Rye whiskey
- Cognac
- Apricot brandy
- Noilly Prat
- Sweet vermouth
- Chambéry vermouth
- Dry vermouth
- Cointreau/Curaçao
- Campari
- Green Chartreuse
- Kahlúa
- Champagne
- Aperol
- Angostura bitters
- Peychaud's bitters
- Selection of liqueurs (amaretto, crème de cacao/menthe, etc.)
- Mandarine Napoléon

Others

- Fresh limes, lemons, oranges, grapefruit
- Coconut cream
- Grenadine
- Freshly squeezed fruit juices
- Purées (peach, banana, mango)
- Maraschino cherries
- Sugar and sugar cubes
- Salt
- Lime cordial
- Tabasco sauce
- Worcestershire sauce
- Gomme syrup
- Simple syrup
- Agave syrup
- Mixers (tonic, soda water, ginger ale, etc.)

MINIBAR SETUP

Once you've developed a passion for mixing drinks, the next thing you'll need is a home bar for assembling them. The days of improvizing in the kitchen will become a thing of the past.

Not all of us have the space to dedicate a corner of a room, let alone an entire room, to mixing drinks. In any case, you can have as much fun making cocktails from a small cocktail cabinet. Look around in fleamarkets or antique shops for them; it's amazing what you can find. The key here is to choose your spirit brands carefully and only buy the spirits and liqueurs that you know you'll use regularly. Because space is limited, restrict the number of spirits to those that work the best with the widest range of cocktails: a good-quality silver or reposado tequila will be more versatile than an expensive añejo, for example.

Store your most useful spirits in the cabinet along with your shaker, strainer, measures, and so on, and keep other less-used spirits and liqueurs close by in a cupboard where you keep your glasses. Store vodka and gin in the fridge so that you also have space in your cabinet for bitters, rum, bourbon/Scotch and tequila.

In a large home bar it is possible to mix a variety of different drinks, but with a smaller setup it might be best to decide what you are going to make in advance. It makes life easier and allows you to concentrate on the most important aspect of mixology, which is making a good drink.

STORAGE

Apart from having the right bottle in the right place at the right time, good storage also involves knowing the best way to preserve a drink's freshness and character.

Spirits

Spirits are less sensitive than wines, but even they have their own peculiarities. White spirits, especially vodka and gin, should be kept in the fridge, or better still in the freezer. The cold temperature gives them a rich texture and, since cocktails are cold drinks, improves the quality of your mixed drink. Remember to stick to brands at 40 per cent ABV (Alcohol By Volume) and above; anything below that will freeze.

Brown spirits, such as brandy, Scotch/bourbon and dark rum, can be kept at room temperature. Unlike wine, spirits do not improve in the bottle, although there are some people who claim that Chartreuse does. Usually a spirit will start to deteriorate if the bottle has been opened months or years before. This is because when air is let into the bottle the spirit starts to oxidize, the aroma flattens and loses its vibrancy. If you do have a half-full bottle of precious malt, cognac or bourbon then simply decant it into a smaller bottle. Brown spirits in clear glass bottles will lose their colour if stored for long periods in direct sunlight.

Wine

Wine storage is a slightly more complex issue. Many wines will improve in the bottle and ideally should be stored in a cellar. That said, most of us tend to drink wine soon after we buy it, which is why many wines are made to be drunk when young. Speak to your wine merchant and find out what wines will benefit from some ageing: these will include quality claret, some Californian and Australian Cabernet and Merlot, Burgundy (red and white), top German Riesling, Loire Chenin Blanc and Cabernet Franc, Rhône reds, Chianti Riserva, Barolo/Barbaresco. The same goes for champagne, including most non-vintage brands. It really is a good idea to buy champagne by the case and store it for a few months.

In the unlikely event...

There are many devices available which aim to preserve wine, but if you are going to finish off the wine the next night, just replace the cork in the bottle. The Vacu Vin system which sucks the air out of the bottle might save the wine from oxidizing but it also sucks the life and aroma out at the same time. Wine bars use a system which pumps nitrogen into the bottle, sealing it from the worst effects of the air, but while it is quite efficient this method is expensive.

There many tips about how to keep champagne, such as putting a silver spoon in the neck of the bottle in order to preserve the bubbles. This is just a myth. Champagne should be sealed with a stopper and placed in the fridge. The stopper won't prevent the gas from escaping – the bubbles remain in the wine for a day or so – but it does prevent any odours from the fridge seeping into the wine.

TECHNIQUES

Shaking

Shaking is the most effective way of mixing the ingredients, while simultaneously chilling the drink and diluting it slightly. Dilution helps to release flavours, allowing them to blend together. Never fill the shaker more than halfway with ice. Shake the drink until the outside of the shaker is freezing to the touch. Cocktails should be very cold. Use ice cubes, not crushed ice, unless otherwise stated in the recipe, because a drink shaken over crushed ice can quickly become too diluted.

Stirring

Stirring is used to marry flavours which go together easily, without making the drink cloudy, which is what happens when you shake. The principle is the same as shaking: a way to mix the ingredients together, chill a drink quickly and dilute it slightly. Half-fill a shaker with ice and stir for about 20 seconds, or until the outside is chilled, then strain into cocktail glasses. Some recipes, for example the Negroni (pages 34–35), suggest the drink is stirred in the serving glasses.

Blending

This is a good way to make long, thirst-quenching drinks. Simply whizz up the ice with the spirit ingredients and serve unstrained in the glass. Because the ice is crushed it melts more quickly and produces a fairly dilute alcoholic slush in the glass. It's a matter of personal preference. Some people like to taste the alcohol in the drink, but can also see the advantage of a frozen blended drink when you have a long, hot summer's afternoon ahead of you and your friends, hence the Frozen Daiquiri.

Muddling

Some recipes, such as the Old-Fashioned, call for "muddling" to take place. This involves pressing and mixing ingredients: mint, fruit, peel, etc. in the bottom of the glass, often with bitters and over sugar cubes. The rough surface of the sugar helps break up the ingredients easily. You can use the back of a spoon if you don't own a proper muddler.

Layering

This process involves introducing the heaviest part of the drink first, followed by a succession of progressively lighter layers. The layers are carefully poured to sit one on top of the other. (See the Horse's Neck, pages 100–101.)

Salting and Sugaring

The intention here is to coat the outside, not the inside, of the rim. Don't, therefore, bury the rim in a pile of salt or sugar. Instead, moisten the outside rim with lime or lemon juice and then carefully turn the glass, side on, in a saucer of salt or sugar. Alternatively, you can sprinkle the salt or sugar onto the rim while rotating the glass, although this is a messier method.

Fruit

When using fruit for a garnish, make sure it is fresh and has been thoroughly washed. Try rolling limes and lemons before you cut them as this starts to release their juices. To cut a twist, pare small strips from a lemon ensuring there is some white pith attached. Holding the peel between thumb and forefinger give it a quick twist so that it sprays some of its oil on the surface of the drink. Run the twist round the rim of the glass and gently drop in.

Flaming

The secret of flaming brandy is to warm the glass first, either over a hot coil on the stove or by holding it under a hot tap. Pour in the brandy and ignite. To light absinthe, or high-proof vodka, hold the flame at the edge of the glass until the alcohol catches. Be aware that the flames can flare up, so ensure that your hair is not hanging over the glass.

Flavoured Spirits

To flavour spirits, simply add the flavouring of your choice – for example, fruit, nuts, peel, chillis, garlic, chocolate or herbs and leave to stand. Vodka is the most widely used base spirit for infusion and since it is light in character, it allows the flavours to show themselves fully. That said, gin is wonderful (think sloe and damson) as is tequila (chilli, even lemon) and overproof rum. You can even use a moscato grappa for a walnut-based infusion and it works well. If you can find high-strength Polish Pure Spirit, use it; the high alcohol level means extraction is quicker. Dilute the result with standard strength vodka. Overproof rum works on the same principle.

You can use sweet or savoury ingredients as flavourings. Do not fall into the trap of using only sweet ingredients: chocolate vodka, for example, is fun the first time you try it, but the novelty soon wears off. Savoury/fresh fruit infusions tend to be more versatile and interesting.

BITTERS

Bitters

Spirits were originally produced to benefit health and there is one branch of the family – bitters – which remain rooted in this ancient purpose. Because of this "drink it, it will do you good" aspect they are regarded with a certain amount of suspicion in the US and the UK. Some are so bitter that drinking them as they come is hardly pleasurable, while making tremendous ingredients for aperitifs or digestifs and essential additions to any home bar.

The bitter ingredient is always vegetal in origin and can come from one or more of the following: quinine/chinchon, angelica, gentian, bitter orange, rue, nux vomica, artichoke, wormwood, bitter aloe or rhubarb root. The potion is then often given a lift by the inclusion of aromatic herbs and spices, similar to gin.

"Medicinal" bitters

These are best taken in small quantities and in one gulp and though claimed to be an aid to digestion, the only use I've ever found for them is as a highly effective cure for an extreme hangover. The best known is the explosive slightly peppermint-accented Fernet-Branca. The German duo Jägermeister and Underberg are equally effective, with the former having a slightly sweeter anise flavour, while Underberg is simply bitter tasting.

Digestif bitters

The best Italian examples are Averna and Montenegro, which are given a boost with sweetened wine. Cynar, whose bitterness comes from artichokes, is relatively light and sweet. Worth trying are Unicum from Hungary and Melnais Balzams from Latvia; both are sweet with the latter having an extra resonance. Spain also has its own versions of these: Chinchon is the most widely seen and occupies a position halfway between a bitters, a liqueur and an anise drink. Better tasting, on that cusp between sweet, herbal and bitter, is Calisay, which also uses chinchona bark as its bittering agent along with herbs, bitter orange and wormwood.

Aperitif bitters

Campari, one of the world's classic drinks, dominates this group of bitters. A gorgeous rich pink colour with lifted aromas of orange and spice, it is one of the great cocktail ingredients as well as a refreshing aperitif. Punt e Mes is halfway between a bitters and a vermouth, as are the French-made Dubonnet and St. Raphaël. France's best bitter-based brand is Suze, which gets its kick from gentian.

Cocktail bitters

There are some bitters which are so intense they only need to be added in minuscule quantities to drinks. The best known is Angostura, created as a cure for malaria but now an essential addition to any bar. It is not the only one of its kind, however. Search for the sweeter anise-flavoured Peychaud from New Orleans or the magnificent Abbot's or Elby orange bitters. If you are in Peru try their variant on the Angostura theme, Amargo. Bitters can turn an ordinary drink into something special.

CITRUS

If there is one thing which separates today's cocktails from the nineteenth- and early twentieth-century classics it is in the extensive use of fruit juices. That's not to say that fruits weren't used in earlier times, for without orange, lemon, lime and grapefruit juice, cocktails just wouldn't have existed. There is one simple rule when it comes to using juice: make sure it is always freshly squeezed. The superiority of freshly squeezed juice over the pre-packaged alternative is obvious and will give the drinks you make added quality. Although many recipes call for "the juice of one lemon", not every lemon contains exactly the same amount of juice, so it is wise to measure the fruit juice accurately rather than just squeezing away.

The more cocktails you make the more you'll need a good juicer to squeeze your own juice. This handy device not only makes excellent health drinks – and allows you to experiment with different combinations of fruit and vegetables – but also opens up all manner of unusual possibilities. One bar in London used its juicer to make a sweet potato juice which was then, believe it or not, used in a bourbon-based cocktail.

Cordials and fruit syrups are also useful items to keep behind your home bar. The best known is grenadine, which is made from pomegranate and is an essential ingredient in rum punches. Rose's Lime Juice cordial is essential for drinks such as the Gimlet (see pages 142–143), while the more elusive, yet wonderfully exotic orgeat (made from almond sugar and rosewater/orange blossom water) lends your drinks an air of sophistication. Use lightly alcoholic fruit cordials such as cassis (blackcurrant) and mûres (blackberry) to give a rich, concentrated fruitiness to drinks.

BITTER
COCKTA

NEGRONI

Bold, bracing, and a bit of a show-off, it's the perfect companion for those moments when you're feeling slightly too fancy for your own good. Stir, sip, and contemplate just how delightful a moment of quiet can be.

Ingredients

- Campari
  1 oz. (30 ml/2 tbsp.)
- Sweet vermouth
  1 oz. (30 ml/2 tbsp.)
- Splash of soda water
  (optional)
- Slice of orange
  to garnish

Method

Over ice, pour the Campari and sweet vermouth into an old-fashioned glass and stir. Add the soda, garnish with the orange slice, and serve.

NEGRONI (ALT)

If you're the sort who believes "why have one when you can have two?", this gin-fortified Negroni variation is just for you. It's like the original but with a little extra punch – perfect for when you're feeling indulgent, or perhaps just indecisive. Let this triple threat remind you that the best things come in balanced measures.

Ingredients

- Gin
  1½ oz. (45 ml/3 tbsp.)
- Campari
  1½ oz. (45 ml/3 tbsp.)
- Sweet vermouth
  1½ oz. (45 ml/3 tbsp.)
- Soda water
  (optional)
- Slice of orange
  to garnish

Method

Shake the ingredients, then pour over ice in a highball glass. Fill with soda, if using, add the garnish, and serve.

VERMOUTH
ROSSO
1863

MANHATTAN

Sophistication in a glass, the Manhattan is for those who prefer their evenings like their whiskey: straight, stirred, and with a dash of drama. It's a cocktail for the thinkers, dreamers, and the occasional cynic who just wants to sip something strong while watching the world spin around them – from a safe distance, naturally.

Ingredients

- Whiskey
  2 oz. (60 ml/4 tbsp.) rye
- Sweet vermouth
  1 oz. (45 ml/3 tbsp.)
- Angostura
  3 dashes
- Drop of maraschino juice
- Maraschino cherry

Method

Stir the ingredients in a mixing glass, then strain into a cocktail glass. Skewer the cherry, add to the glass and serve.

EAST HARLEM

Swap the rye for tequila and suddenly you're on a holiday, even if you're just sitting at home in your pyjamas. The East Harlem is a sultry twist on the classic Manhattan, like wearing sunglasses indoors. Bold, unexpected, and a little bit spicy – just like the nights you'll have with this one in hand.

Ingredients

- Tequila
  2 oz. (60 ml/4 tbsp.)
- Sweet vermouth
  1 oz. (30 ml/2 tbsp.)
- Dash of fresh lime juice
- Chilli pepper
  to garnish

Method

Shake the ingredients, then strain into an ice-filled old-fashioned glass. Cut off the top end of the chilli pepper, place stem upwards in the drink to garnish, and serve.

MEXICO
TEQUILA
HANDCRAFTED FROM AGAVE AZUL

PALOMA

Feeling zesty? The Paloma is the grapefruit lover's answer to "what's life without a little fizz?" Light, refreshing, and wonderfully tart, it's the perfect companion when you're longing for a sunny escape but settling for your balcony. A slice of tropical paradise, just for you – because why should margaritas have all the fun?

Ingredients

- Tequila
  2 oz. (60 ml/4 tbsp.)
- Grapefruit juice
  2 oz. (60 ml/4 tbsp.)
- Agave syrup
  1 oz. (30 ml/2 tbsp.)
- Juice of 1 lime
- Soda water
- Slice of grapefruit
  to garnish

Method

Shake all of the ingredients, except the soda water, in a shaker with ice. Strain into a salt-rimmed margarita glass. Top with the soda water, garnish with the grapefruit slice and serve.

APEROL SPRITZ

When life gives you lemons, you should really demand oranges. This effervescent beauty is the epitome of effortless chic, just like you after your first glass. It's light, it's bright, and it's the perfect excuse to pretend you're in Italy, even if the only view you've got is your neighbour's laundry.

Ingredients

- Aperol
  3 oz. (90 ml/6 tbsp.)
- Dry Prosecco
  3 oz. (90 ml/6 tbsp.)
- Soda
  1 oz. (30 ml/2 tbsp.)
- Orange slice
  to garnish

Method

Fill a wine glass with ice. Add the aperol and Prosecco, top with the soda and garnish with the orange slice before serving.

MILANO
LIQUEUR

CAMPARI SPRITZ

For the bitter souls who need a bit of sparkle, the Campari Spritz is here to save the day. Think of it as the Aperol Spritz's edgier cousin – still bubbly, but with a sharp bite that says, "I'm here to be noticed." Best enjoyed when you want to feel classy, yet slightly rebellious.

Ingredients

- Campari
  3 oz. (90 ml/6 tbsp.)
- Dry Prosecco
  3 oz. (90 ml/6 tbsp.)
- Soda
  1 oz. (30 ml/2 tbsp.)
- Orange slice
  to garnish
- Orange zest
  to serve

Method

Fill a wine glass with ice. Add the Campari and Prosecco, top with the soda and garnish with the orange slice and zest before serving.

SAZERAC

A drink with history and swagger, the Sazerac isn't for the faint-hearted. It's bold, boozy, and a little bit mysterious – much like you after a few sips. With a touch of absinthe, it's perfect for when you're feeling a bit more daring.

Ingredients

- Bourbon
  2½ oz. (75 ml/5 tbsp.)
- Absinthe or Pernod
  2 tsp.
- Gomme Syrup
  ½ tsp.
- Peychaud's bitters
  3 dashes
- Twist of lemon
  to garnish

Method

Pour the bourbon and absinthe/Pernod into a highball glass, coat, and discard the excess. Shake the other ingredients and pour over ice into the glass, then serve with a twist of lemon.

AUTHENTIC

OLD-FASHIONED

The Old-Fashioned is the granddaddy of cocktails – timeless, reliable, and unapologetically strong. It's for those nights when you need a drink that says, "I've seen it all, and I'm still here." Sip slowly, stir thoughtfully, and let this classic remind you that some things never go out of style.

Ingredients

- Angostura bitters
  3 dashes
- 1 sugar cube
- Bourbon
  3 oz. (90 ml/6 tbsp.)
- Ice cubes
- Slice of orange
- Orange slice and Maraschino cherry
  to garnish

Method

Put the bitters, sugar cube, and a dash of the bourbon into an old-fashioned glass and muddle. Add two ice cubes and 2 tablespoons of the bourbon and stir. Squeeze some of the juice from the orange slice into the glass, then add two more ice cubes and 2 more tablespoons of the bourbon and stir again. Finally, add two more ice cubes and the remaining bourbon. Garnish with the orange slice and the cherry.

ESPRESSO MARTINI

The perfect mix of pick-me-up and slow-me-down, ideal for those late nights when you're the last ones standing. A bit of caffeine, a touch of vodka – cheers to staying awake for the fun!

Ingredients

- Vodka
  2 oz. (60 ml/4 tbsp.)
- Kahlúa
  1 oz. (30 ml/2 tbsp.)
- Espresso
  1 oz. (30 ml/2 tbsp.)
- 3 whole coffee beans

Method

Fill a cocktail shaker with ice cubes, then add the vodka, Kahlúa and espresso. Shake well before straining into a cocktail glass and garnish with the three coffee beans before serving.

WHISKY
EST
1879

SCOTCH MARTINI

The drink for when you want to feel a bond with something other than your sofa. Scotch whisky mingling with both sweet and dry vermouths makes this cocktail sophisticated yet approachable, much like you on a good day. It's the perfect drink to remind you that balance is everything.

Ingredients

- Scotch whisky
  2 oz. (60 ml/4 tbsp.)
- Sweet vermouth
  1½ oz. (45 ml/3 tbsp.)
- Dry vermouth
  1½ oz. (45 ml/3 tbsp.)
- Twist of lemon
  to garnish

Method

Stir the whisky and vermouths in a mixing glass, then strain into a martini glass and serve with the lemon twist.

ROAD TRIP

The ultimate escape from everyday life (and responsibility), this cocktail will certainly send your tastebuds on a joyride. With Campari, tequila, and a hint of Cointreau all shaken up with egg white, it's a drink that says, "I'm going places."

Ingredients

- Campari
  1 oz. (30 ml/2 tbsp.)
- Tequila
  1 oz. (30 ml/2 tbsp.)
- Cointreau
  ½ oz. (15 ml/1 tbsp.)
- 1 egg white

Method

Shake the ingredients, then strain into a cocktail glass and serve.

ROSALITA

The Rosalita is a delightful enigma – a little bit sweet, a little bit bitter, and entirely intoxicating. With tequila, vermouths and Campari, it's like a bouquet of flavours from across the sweet and bitter spectrum, celebrating the different sides of yourself. Sip slowly and savour. Here's to you.

Ingredients

- Tequila
  ¾ oz. (22 ml/1 ½ tbsp.)
- Dry vermouth
  ¼ oz. (8 ml/ ½ tbsp.)
- Sweet vermouth
  ¼ oz. (8 ml/ ½ tbsp.)
- Campari
  ¼ oz. (8 ml/ ½ tbsp.)

Method

Shake the ingredients, then strain into a martini glass and serve.

NOVARA SUNRISE

If you and your friends are reaching for cocktails at sunrise, you might have had quite the night. This gin and Campari concoction, brightened by fresh orange juice, is here to welcome the new day with open arms. Cheers to new beginnings – or at least to surviving last night.

Ingredients

- Gin
  1 oz. (30 ml/2 tbsp.)
- Campari
  ⅔ oz. (20 ml/1 ⅓ tbsp.)
- Fresh orange juice
  1⅔ oz. (50 ml/3 ⅓ tbsp.)

Method

Shake the ingredients, then strain into an old-fashioned glass over crushed ice and serve.

DUE CAMPARI

For when one Campari simply isn't enough, we present the Due Campari – a double dose of bitter elegance, softened by a splash of champagne. It's the drink for when you're feeling extra, but still sophisticated.

Ingredients

- Fresh lemon juice
  ¾ oz. (22 ml/1½ tbsp.)
- Campari
  ¼ oz. (8 ml/½ tbsp.)
- Cordiale Campari
  ¾ oz. (22 ml/1½ tbsp.)
- Champagne

Method

Shake the lemon juice and both Camparis, then strain into a champagne flute. Fill with champagne, stir, and serve.

FILBY

The Filby is the cocktail equivalent of that stylish friend who always seems to know what's cool before everyone else. With gin, Campari, dry vermouth, and a cheeky splash of amaretto, it's a drink that's both sharp and sweet – like your wit. Best enjoyed when you're feeling a bit mysterious and in need of a strong, stylish companion.

Ingredients

- Gin
  2 oz. (60 ml/4 tbsp.)
- Campari
  1 oz. (30 ml/2 tbsp.)
- Dry vermouth
  1 oz. (30 ml/2 tbsp.)
- Amaretto
  1 oz. (30 ml/2 tbsp.)

Method

Stir the ingredients in a mixing glass, then strain into an old-fashioned glass and serve.

ORIGINALE
SINCE 1795

AMERICANO SPUMANTE

Like its caffeinated namesake, the Americano Spumante is here to perk you up – but with far more fizz. Campari and sweet vermouth meet sparkling wine in this classic bubbly delight. It's the drink for those moments when you need a bit of sparkle in your life, starting with your glass.

Ingredients

- Campari
  1 oz. (30 ml/2 tbsp.)
- Sweet vermouth
  ½ oz. (15 ml/1 tbsp.)
- Champagne or Prosecco
  (Italian sparkling wine)
- Lime slice
  to garnish

Method

Shake the ingredients, then pour over ice in a highball glass. Fill up with champagne or Prosecco, add the lime, and serve.

JAPONICA

The Japonica is like a cocktail treasure hunt – with vodka, gin, kumquat, and a splash of nearly everything else you've got in the cupboard. It's a complex blend for the drinker who likes their cocktails with a side of mystery. Sip thoughtfully, and let this eclectic mix remind you that sometimes, the best things come in unexpected combinations.

Ingredients

- Splash Cointreau
- Splash Campari
- Ketel One vodka
  1 oz. (30 ml/2 tbsp.)
- Bombay Sapphire gin
  ¾ oz. (22 ml/1 ½ tbsp.)
- Caravella
  ¾ oz. (22 ml/1 ½ tbsp.)
- Candied kumquat nectar
  1 tsp.
- Twist of lemon
  to garnish
- Twist of kumquat
  to garnish

Method

Coat the shaker with the Cointreau and Campari, and then discard the excess. Shake the rest of the ingredients, then strain into a cocktail glass and serve with the garnish.

GIADA

The Giada is a sultry, exotic affair – a blend of vodka, Campari, Galliano and pineapple juice that feels like a holiday in a glass. It's for the nights when you need a bit of escapism, or perhaps just a reminder that you're far more glamorous than your current surroundings suggest. Serve with a smile, a sense of adventure and perhaps searching for your next trip...

Ingredients

- Vodka
  1 oz. (30 ml/2 tbsp.)
- Campari
  ½ oz. (15 ml/1 tbsp.)
- Galliano
  ½ oz. (15 ml/1 tbsp.)
- Dash pineapple juice

Method

Shake the ingredients, then strain into an old-fashioned glass and serve.

BITTER PEACH

This one's for the bourbon lovers who like their drinks with a side of peachy sweetness and a hint of rebellion. Bitter Peach rings in the good times with bourbon, peach schnapps, and a dash of Campari. It's the perfect combination, just like you, your sofa, a friend and your favourite old movie.

Ingredients

- Bourbon
  2 oz. (60 ml/4 tbsp.)
- Peach Schnapps
  1 oz. (30 ml/2 tbsp.)
- Dash apricot brandy
- Dash Campari

Method

Stir the ingredients in a mixing glass, then strain into a martini glass and serve.

SCHNAPPS
PEACH
SCHNAPPS

BELLA, BELLA

Ah, Bella, Bella – a cocktail so lovely, they named it twice. With gin, Aperol, limoncello, and a hint of mandarin, it's like an Italian holiday in a glass. Sip this beauty and let the bitter-citrusy goodness transport you somewhere sun-kissed and glamorous.

Ingredients

- Gin
  1 oz. (30 ml/2 tbsp.)
- Aperol
  ⅔ oz. (20 ml/1 ⅓ tbsp.)
- Limoncello
  ½ oz. (15 ml/1 tbsp.)
- Mandarin liqueur
  ½ oz. (15 ml/1 tbsp.)
- Fresh orange juice
  ⅔ oz. (20 ml/1 ⅓ tbsp.)
- Lime spiral
  to garnish

Method

Shake the ingredients, then strain into a martini glass. Add the lime spiral and serve.

OLD VERMOUTH

If you're feeling nostalgic for a time you never actually lived through, the Old Vermouth is here to indulge your inner old soul. With Old Tom gin and a balanced blend of vermouths, this cocktail is the perfect companion for reminiscing over past lives – or just past episodes of your favourite show. Classy, yet delightfully approachable.

Ingredients

- Old Tom gin
  1 oz. (30 ml/2 tbsp.)
- Dry vermouth
  1 oz. (30 ml/2 tbsp.)
- Sweet vermouth
  ½ oz. (15 ml/1 tbsp.)
- Angostura bitters
  2 dashes
- 2 cocktail cherries
  to garnish

Method

Pour the ingredients into an old-fashioned glass and stir. Garnish with the skewered cherries and serve.

CHARTREUSE

The Chartreuse is unsurprisingly cool and crisp like its namesake shade, with gin and a splash of this yellow liqueur delivering a drink that's as mysterious as the northern lights. It's a cocktail for those who enjoy their drink with a twist of lemon and a dash of something a bit exotic. Perfect for some joyful escapism.

Ingredients

- Gin
  2 oz. (60 ml/4 tbsp.)
- Splash yellow Chartreuse
- Dash Angostura or orange bitters
- Lemon twist
  to garnish

Method

Shake the ingredients, then strain into a martini glass. Add the twist and serve.

OLD OSAKA

East meets West in this elegant, Japanese twist on a classic. The smooth depth of Hibiki whisky paired with the herbal notes of Benedictine creates a sophisticated sipper. A dash of orange bitters adds just the right zing. Served in a martini glass, it's understated luxury in liquid form – perfect for those who appreciate the finer things.

Ingredients

- Hibiki whisky
  2 oz. (60 ml/4 tbsp.)
- Benedictine
  1 oz. (30 ml/2 tbsp.)
- Dash orange bitters

Method

Shake the ingredients, then strain into a martini glass and serve.

WHISKEY

Dry Vermouth
PRODUCT OF GREAT BRITAIN

ALFONZO

The Alfonzo is a cocktail with grand aspirations – a bit like you after a couple of these. With Grand Marnier, gin and vermouths, it's a sophisticated blend that demands your full attention. A drink fit for the discerning drinker who appreciates the finer things in life.

Ingredients

- Grand Marnier
  2 oz. (60 ml/4 tbsp.)
- Gin
  1 oz. (30 ml/2 tbsp.)
- Dry vermouth
  1 oz. (30 ml/2 tbsp.)
- Sweet vermouth
  ½ oz. (15 ml/1 tbsp.)
- Dash Angostura bitters

Method

Shake the ingredients, then strain into a martini glass and serve.

ALGONQUIN

Named after the hotel that hosted some of history's wittiest minds, the Algonquin is a cocktail that's both sharp and playful. With rye whiskey, dry vermouth, and pineapple juice, it's the perfect blend of sweet and strong. Sip it and imagine you're exchanging quips with Dorothy Parker.

Ingredients

- Rye whiskey
  2 oz. (60 ml/4 tbsp.)
- Dry vermouth
  1 oz. (30 ml/2 tbsp.)
- Pineapple juice
  1 oz. (30 ml/2 tbsp.)
- Dash of Peychaud bitters

Method

Shake the ingredients, then strain into a martini glass and serve.

ANGLO ANGEL

The Anglo Angel is a heavenly blend of vodka, Mandarine Napoléon, and mandarin juice – a cocktail for when you're feeling virtuous but still want a bit of mischief. The Angostura bitters add just the right amount of devilish charm. Best enjoyed with a halo that's slightly askew, and perhaps a cheeky grin to match.

Ingredients

- Vodka
  1 oz. (30 ml/2 tbsp.)
- Mandarine Napoléon
  1 oz. (30 ml/2 tbsp.)
- Mandarin juice
  1 oz. (30 ml/2 tbsp.)
- Angostura bitters
  3 dashes

Method

Shake the ingredients, then strain into a martini glass and serve.

SAKETINI

If James Bond had ever ventured to Tokyo, he'd have ordered this. A delightful fusion of gin's crispness and sake's subtle elegance, the Saketini is the martini's cooler, more refined cousin. Stirred, not shaken – because we're classy like that – this drink is the ideal choice when you're looking for a twist on a classic.

Ingredients

- Gin
  3 oz. (90 ml/6 tbsp.)
- Sake
  1 oz. (30 ml/2 tbsp.)
- Angostura bitters
  3 dashes
- Lemon slice
  to garnish

Method

Stir the ingredients in a mixing glass, then strain into a martini glass and serve with a lemon slice.

水代

GIN

ASTORIA

The Astoria is a drink that exudes old-world charm – think grand hotel lobbies, clinking glasses, and whispered secrets. With gin, dry vermouth, and a dash of orange bitters, it's the cocktail equivalent of a perfectly tailored suit. Enjoy this classic concoction when you're feeling especially dapper.

Ingredients

- Gin
  2 oz. (60 ml/4 tbsp.)
- Dry vermouth
  1 oz. (30 ml/2 tbsp.)
- Dash orange bitters

Method

Shake the ingredients, then strain into a cocktail glass and serve.

SLOE EVENING

For when the night calls for something rich and smooth, the Sloe Evening delivers. Combining the fruity warmth of sloe gin with the sharp edge of classic gin, this cocktail strikes the perfect balance between sweet and dry. A dash of Angostura bitters gives just the right amount of intrigue, making it the ideal companion for unwinding after a cold winter's day.

Ingredients

- Sloe gin
  2 oz. (60 ml/4 tbsp.)
- Gin
  1 oz. (30 ml/2 tbsp.)
- dash Angostura bitters

Method

Shake the ingredients, then strain into a martini glass and serve.

DANDY

For those nights when you feel like donning a monocle and twirling your metaphorical moustache, the Dandy is your go-to drink. With Dubonnet, bourbon, and a hint of Cointreau, it's a cocktail that exudes old-school charm with a dash of mystery. Shake it up, sip it down, and remember: it's always dapper to drink from a martini glass.

Ingredients

- Dubonnet
  2 oz. (60 ml/4 tbsp.)
- Bourbon
  1 oz. (30 ml/2 tbsp.)
- Cointreau
  1 oz. (30 ml/2 tbsp.)
- Dash Angostura bitters

Method

Shake the ingredients, then strain into a martini glass and serve.

H. G. WELLS

If you're feeling a bit literary, why not raise a glass to H. G. Wells? This bourbon-based cocktail with a touch of Pernod is a perfect blend of sophistication and intrigue. Best enjoyed while pondering time travel, alien invasions, or simply the mysteries of your own existence. One sip, and you'll be ready to write your own future – or at least your next drink order.

Ingredients

- Bourbon
  2 oz. (60 ml/4 tbsp.)
- Dry vermouth
  1 oz. (30 ml/2 tbsp.)
- Pernod
  ½ oz. (15 ml/1 tbsp.)
- Angostura bitters
  2 dashes

Method

Stir the ingredients in a mixing glass, then strain into an ice-filled old-fashioned glass and serve.

HARMONY

The drink that brings balance to your glass, if not your life. Cognac and crème de fraises create a sweet symphony, with a dash of maraschino liqueur adding a high note, and a touch of orange bitterness. Stir it up and let the flavours play in perfect harmony. Ideal for when you need a little something extra-sweet.

Ingredients

- Cognac
  2 oz. (60 ml/4 tbsp.)
- Crème de fraises
  ½ oz. (15 ml/1 tbsp.)
- Orange bitters
  2 dashes
- Dash maraschino liqueur

Method

Stir the ingredients in an old-fashioned glass and serve over ice.

HORSE'S NECK

Don't let the name fool you, the Horse's Neck is far more refined than its equine title suggests. With bourbon, bitters and ginger ale, it's a spirited drink that trots between bold and refreshing. The twist of lemon adds a dash of elegance, making this cocktail the perfect companion for a relaxed evening – no training reins required.

Ingredients

- Angostura bitters
  2 dashes
- Bourbon
  2 oz. (60 ml/4 tbsp.)
- Gin
  1 oz. (30 ml/2 tbsp.)
- Ginger ale
- Twist of lemon

Method

Coat a highball glass with bitters. Add ice and the bourbon and gin. Stir, then fill with ginger ale and the lemon twist. Stir briefly and serve.

MONTE
STAMBECCO
ITALY
MARASCHINO
CHERRY AMARO

IMPERIAL

Feel like royalty? The Imperial cocktail will crown your evening with gin, dry vermouth, and a hint of maraschino liqueur. It's a drink that rules with a light touch, perfect for those who prefer their power in a glass rather than on a throne. Sip regally and feel like an emperor.

Ingredients

- Gin
  1 oz. (30 ml/2 tbsp.)
- Dry vermouth
  1 oz. (30 ml/2 tbsp.)
- Dash maraschino liqueur
- Dash Angostura bitters

Method

Shake the ingredients, then strain into a martini glass and serve.

LONDON COCKTAIL

The London Cocktail is as sharp and sophisticated as the city itself. With London dry gin, maraschino liqueur, and a dash of bitters, it's a drink that's both classic and cosmopolitan. Shake it up and savour the taste of the capital – from a Kensington rooftop to a Dalston dive bar and everything in between. Perfect for when you need a bit of London flair, no matter where you are.

Ingredients

- London dry gin
  2 oz. (60 ml/4 tbsp.)
- Dash maraschino liqueur
- Orange bitters
  2 dashes
- Dash gomme syrup

Method

Shake the ingredients, then strain into a cocktail glass and serve.

NINETEEN

If you're feeling a bit nostalgic for your wilder days, the Nineteen cocktail will take you back – but with far more class. Dry vermouth, kirsch and gin combine for a sophisticated sip, while a hint of gomme syrup smooths it out. Shake it up, sip slowly, and toast to the fact that you're older, wiser, and still know how to enjoy a good drink.

Ingredients

- Dry vermouth
  2 oz. (60 ml/4 tbsp.)
- Kirsch
  ½ oz. (15 ml/1 tbsp.)
- Gin
  ½ oz. (15 ml/1 tbsp.)
- Angostura bitters
  2 dashes
- Gomme syrup
  ½ oz. (15 ml/1 tbsp.)

Method

Shake the ingredients, then strain into a martini glass or coupe and serve.

PAN-AM

The Pan-Am is a transcontinental journey in a glass, blending bourbon and mescal for a smoky, adventurous flavour. It's a drink that evokes the golden age of travel, even if you're miles away from air miles. Pour yourself a glass, stir and let your tastebuds take flight – no passport required.

Ingredients

- Bourbon
  1 oz. (30 ml/2 tbsp.)
- Mescal
  1 oz. (30 ml/2 tbsp.)
- Dash Angostura bitters
- Dash gomme syrup

Method

Pour the ingredients into an old-fashioned glass, stir, and serve.

SEELBACH COCKTAIL

Fourteen dashes of bitters? You're not messing around. The Seelbach Cocktail combines bourbon, Cointreau, and champagne for a drink that's as bold as it's bubbly. This is the drink for when you're feeling particularly daring – or just in need of a bit of sparkle in your life. Garnish with an orange twist and prepare to impress.

Ingredients

- Old Forester bourbon
  1 oz. (30 ml/2 tbsp.)
- Cointreau
  ½ oz. (15 ml/1 tbsp.)
- Angostura bitters
  7 dashes
- Peychaud orange bitters
  7 dashes
- Champagne
  5 oz. (120 ml/10 tbsp.)
- Twist of orange
  to garnish

Method

Pour the bourbon, Cointreau, and both bitters into a champagne flute and stir. Add the champagne, stir, garnish with the twist of orange, and serve.

TART
COCKTA

CASABLANCA

Here's looking at you, cocktail connoisseur. The Casablanca is a classic rum cocktail with Cointreau, lime juice, and a hint of bitters – perfect for those nights when you want to channel your inner Humphrey Bogart. Shake it up, strain it into a martini glass, and imagine yourself in a faraway land – because of all the cocktails in all the world, this is the one for you.

Ingredients

- White rum
  2 oz. (60 ml/4 tbsp.)
- Cointreau
  1 oz. (30 ml/2 tbsp.)
- Fresh lime juice
  1 oz. (30 ml/2 tbsp.)
- Dash orange bitters
- Dash Maraschino liqueur (optional)

Method

Shake the ingredients, then strain into a martini glass and serve.

JOHN COLLINS

Meet John Collins, the bourbon-forward cousin of the Tom Collins. With a foundation of smooth bourbon, bright lemon juice and a touch of sugar, this refreshing highball cocktail is a balanced blend of sweet, tart, and spirited. Topped with a splash of soda and optional bitters for complexity, it's a laid-back drink that's just as perfect for sunny afternoons as it is for cosy cool evenings.

Ingredients

- Bourbon
  2 oz. (60 ml/4 tbsp.)
- Lemon juice
  1 oz. (30 ml/2 tbsp.)
- Superfine (caster) sugar
  1 tsp.
- Dash Angostura bitters
  (optional)
- Soda
- Lemon slice to garnish

Method

Place the first three ingredients in a highball glass, half-filled with ice, and stir. Fill up with soda. Stir gently and serve garnished with a lemon slice.

AGAVE SOUR

The Agave Sour is a vibrant twist on a classic sour, blending the earthiness of silver tequila with a hint of tropical pineapple juice. Angostura bitters add complexity, while a splash of soda lightens it up. Served over ice and garnished with a pineapple leaf, this refreshing cocktail is perfect for those who like their drinks crisp, flavourful and full of zest.

Ingredients

- Silver tequila
  2 oz. (60 ml/4 tbsp.)
- Pineapple juice
  2 tsp.
- Angostura bitters
  3 dashes
- Club soda
- Pineapple leaf
  to garnish

Method

Pour the ingredients, except the soda, into an ice-filled old-fashioned glass. Stir. Fill with soda. Stir. Add the pineapple leaf and serve.

PISCO SOUR

The Pisco Sour is a drink with a bit of flair – and by flair, we mean egg white (optional, of course). This South American classic is tart, tasty and just the right amount of smooth. Shake it like you mean it. It's the perfect cocktail to impress the most important person in any room – yourself.

Ingredients

- Gran Pisco
  2 oz. (60 ml/4 tbsp.)
- Lemon juice
  1 oz. (30 ml/2 tbsp.)
- Superfine (caster) sugar
  1 tsp.
- Egg white
  (optional)
- Bitters
  to garnish (optional)

Method

Shake the ingredients well, particularly if you are using an egg white, then strain into a cocktail glass, garnish with a dash of bitters and serve.

SINGAPORE SLING

Fancy a cocktail with a bit of history and a lot of panache? The Singapore Sling is a journey in a glass, taking you from gin-soaked beginnings to tropical tang with lime and cherry. It's bold, it's colourful, and it's just the right mix of sweet and sour. Perfect for when you want that holiday vibe without leaving your front door.

Ingredients

- Beefeater gin
  2 oz. (60 ml/4 tbsp.)
- Fresh lime juice
  2 oz. (60 ml/4 tbsp.)
- Dash of Angostura bitters
- Cointreau
  ½ oz. (15 ml/1 tbsp.)
- Peter Heering
  ½ oz. (15 ml/1 tbsp.)
- Sugar
  2 tsp.
- Soda
- Red maraschino cherry
  to garnish

Method

Pour the gin, lime juice, and bitters over crushed ice in a highball glass. Add the sugar and stir. Then add the Cointreau and Peter Heering, fill up with soda, and serve with a maraschino cherry.

TOM COLLINS

The Tom Collins is the drink equivalent of a stiff upper lip – refreshing, classic, and just a bit proper. With gin, lemon juice and a splash of soda, it's the kind of cocktail that doesn't need to shout to be heard. Stir gently, sip leisurely and remind yourself that some things – like this drink, and you – never go out of style.

Ingredients

- Gin
  2 oz. (60 ml/4 tbsp.)
- Fresh lemon juice
  1 oz. (30 ml/2 tbsp.)
- Superfine (caster) sugar
  1 tsp.
- Dash Angostura bitters (optional)
- Soda

Method

Place the first three ingredients in an ice-filled highball glass, then stir to mix. Add a dash of bitters if liked. Fill up with soda. Stir gently and serve.

TROPICAL STORM

This fruity concoction is a whirlwind of flavours – orange, lime, pineapple, and a dash of grenadine to keep things interesting. Blend it up, pour it out, and let the storms of life pass while you sip your way to paradise, one delightful mouthful at a time.

Ingredients

- Golden rum
  2 oz. (60 ml/4 tbsp.)
- Vodka
  1 oz. (30 ml/2 tbsp.)
- Fresh orange juice
  1 oz. (30 ml/2 tbsp.)
- Fresh lime juice
  ½ oz. (15 ml/1 tbsp.)
- Pineapple juice
  ½ oz. (15 ml/1 tbsp.)
- Dash grenadine
- Dash Angostura bitters and a lemon slice
  to garnish

Method

Blend the ingredients until smooth, then pour into an ice-filled highball glass and serve with bitters and a twist of lemon.

MAPLE SYRUP
ORGANIC

WOODSTOCK

Maple syrup in a cocktail? Absolutely – Woodstock is the sweet and sour rebellion in a glass. Gin, lemon juice, and a dash of bitters join forces with that Canadian staple, proving that a little syrup goes a long way. Shake it up, serve it in a martini glass, and let your tastebuds embrace the groovy side of life.

Ingredients

- Gin
  1 oz. (30 ml/2 tbsp.)
- Lemon juice
  1 oz. (30 ml/2 tbsp.)
- Maple syrup
  1 tsp.
- Dash Angostura bitters

Method

Shake the ingredients, then strain into a martini glass and serve.

A1

Why settle for anything less than A1? This gin-based cocktail with Grand Marnier and a hint of lemon is top-shelf in every sense. It's crisp, citrusy and sophisticated. Shake, strain and sip your way to first-class satisfaction.

Ingredients

- Gin
  2 oz. (60 ml/4 tbsp.)
- Grand Marnier
  1 oz. (30 ml/2 tbsp.)
- Dash fresh lemon juice
- Sugar
  2 tsp.
- Twist of lemon
  to serve

Method

Shake the ingredients, then strain into a sugar-rimmed cocktail glass, garnish, and serve.

ALABAMA FIZZ

If a Southern drawl could be turned into a cocktail, it would be the Alabama Fizz. Gin and lemon juice meet soda for a drink that's as refreshing as a front porch in summer. Simple, classic and just a little bit fizzy – it's the perfect companion for when you want to take it easy, one slow sip at a time.

Ingredients

- Gin
  2 oz. (60 ml/4 tbsp.)
- Fresh lemon juice
  1 oz. (30 ml/2 tbsp.)
- Dash gomme syrup
- Club soda
- Lemon slices
  to garnish

Method

Shake the ingredients, except the soda, then strain into an ice-filled highball glass. Fill with soda, stir, and serve garnished with lemon slices.

SOUR CHERRY MARTINI

The Sour Cherry Martini is a tantalizing blend of bright, tart lemon juice and the subtle sweetness of maraschino liqueur, all balanced by a smooth vodka base. Shaken to perfection and garnished with maraschino cherries, this cocktail is both vibrant and elegant, offering a refreshing burst of flavour with every sip. Perfect for those who love a sweet-tart twist on the classic martini.

Ingredients

- Vodka
  12/3 oz. (50 ml/11/3 tbsp.)
- Maraschino liqueur
  1 oz. (30 ml/2 tbsp.)
- Fresh lemon juice
  2/3 oz. (20 ml/11/3 tbsp.)
- Maraschino cherries
  to garnish

Method

Shake the ingredients, then strain into a cocktail glass. Spear the cherries on a cocktail stick to garnish, and serve.

BLOOD ORANGE MARGARITA

Elevate the Margarita with a juicy twist of fresh citrus. This tequila-forward classic with Cointreau is the perfect balance of sour and sweet, with a salt-rimmed glass to keep things interesting. Whether you're celebrating something special or just the end of the week, shake it up, strain it out and let the fiesta begin.

Ingredients

- Gold tequila
  2 oz. (60 ml/4 tbsp.)
- Cointreau or triple sec
  1 oz. (30 ml/2 tbsp.)
- Juice of half a lime
- Juice of half a blood orange
- Citrus slices
  to garnish

Method

Shake the ingredients, then strain into a salt-rimmed margarita glass and serve garnished with citrus slices.

FROZEN MARGARITA

Why limit happy to just an hour when you've got a Frozen Margarita? This icy blend of tequila, Cointreau, and fresh citrus is your ticket to a frosty fiesta. Whether you keep it classic or add your favourite fruit for a twist, this cocktail is perfect for cooling down on a hot day – or turning any day into a celebration. Don't forget the spicy rim!

Ingredients

- Tequila
  2 oz. (60 ml/4 tbsp.)
- Cointreau
  1 oz. (30 ml/2 tbsp.)
- Juice of half a lime, plus an extra squeeze for the rim
- Juice of half a lemon
- Tajin seasoning
- Lime slice
  to garnish

Method

Wipe the rim of a margarita glass with lime juice, and then dip in the Tajin seasoning to coat the rim. Blend the ingredients with crushed ice until frozen, then pour into the margarita glass. Serve garnished with lime slices.

DAIQUIRI

Simple, elegant, and timeless – the Daiquiri is proof that less really is more. White rum, lime juice, and a touch of sugar come together in this classic cocktail that's as refreshing as a breeze on a tropical beach. Shake it up, strain it out and let the tart, sweet perfection take you to your happy place.

Ingredients

- White rum
  2 oz. (60 ml/4 tbsp.)
- Juice of 1 lime
- Sugar
  1 tsp.
- Lemon twist
  to garnish
- Non-edible flower (optional)
  to garnish

Method

Shake the ingredients, then strain into a cocktail glass, add the garnish, and serve.

GIMLET

Simplicity never tasted so good. Whether you prefer gin or vodka, the Gimlet's blend of spirit and lime cordial is a classic for a reason. Served over ice with a wedge of lime, it's the kind of drink that's as straightforward as it is satisfying. Perfect for those who like their cocktails with a twist – but not too much fuss.

Ingredients

- Gin or vodka
  2 oz. (60 ml/4 tbsp.)
- Lime cordial
  1 oz. (30 ml/2 tbsp.)
- Wedge of lime
  to garnish

Method

Pour the spirit and lime cordial over ice cubes in an old-fashioned glass and serve with a lime wedge.

WHISKY SOUR

Bold and balanced, the Whisky Sour is a cocktail that knows how to make an impression. Whisky, lemon juice and gomme syrup come together in a drink that's equal parts tart and smooth, with just the right amount of bite. Shake it up, pour it out and enjoy a classic that never goes out of style.

Ingredients

- Whisky
  2 oz. (60 ml/4 tbsp.)
- Fresh lemon juice
  1 oz. (30 ml/2 tbsp.)
- Gomme syrup
  ½ oz. (15 ml/1 tbsp.)

Method

Shake the whisky, lemon juice, and syrup, then pour into a cocktail glass and serve.

COSMOPOLITAN

If you couldn't help but wonder how to channel your inner Carrie Bradshaw or you're just in the mood for something chic, the Cosmopolitan has you covered. Vodka, Cointreau, lime and cranberry juice make this cocktail the epitome of '90s cool. Stir it up, strain it into a chilled glass, and let the retro vibes take hold.

Ingredients

- Vodka
  2 oz. (60 ml/4 tbsp.)
- Cointreau
  1 oz. (30 ml/2 tbsp.)
- Lime juice
  ½ oz. (15 ml/1 tbsp.)
- Splash cranberry juice
- Lime twist
  to garnish

Method

Stir the ingredients in a mixing glass, then strain into a chilled martini glass. Garnish with the lime twist and serve.

BLOODY MARY

The Bloody Mary is the breakfast of champions – or at least, the brunch of champions. Vodka, tomato juice and a dash of spice make this cocktail the go-to cure for whatever ails you. Whether you like it mild or with a kick, this savoury sipper is sure to wake up your tastebuds.

Ingredients

- Vodka
  2 oz. (60 ml/4 tbsp.)
- Tomato juice
  6 oz. (180 ml/8 tbsp.)
- Worcestershire sauce
  2 dashes
- Pinch black pepper
- Pinch of celery salt
- Fresh lemon juice
  ½ oz. (15 ml/1 tbsp.)
- Tabasco sauce
  to taste

Method

Pour the vodka over ice in a highball glass. Combine the other ingredients in a jug, then add the mix to the vodka. (A celery stick garnish and lime slice are optional!)

AMARETTO SOUR

Gin and amaretto get a tart kick from fresh lemon juice, while an egg white smooths things out like a well-timed witticism. Shaken to perfection and served with an air of sophistication, it's the kind of drink that can make any moment feel a jot more refined.

Ingredients

- Gin
  1 oz. (30 ml/2 tbsp.)
- Amaretto
  1 oz. (30 ml/2 tbsp.)
- Fresh lemon juice
  1 oz. (30 ml/2 tbsp.)
- 1 egg white
- Lemon slice and cocktail cherry
  to garnish

Method

Shake the ingredients, then strain into a martini glass and serve with a lemon slice and cherry.

CLOVER CLUB

A cocktail that's as pretty as it is delicious, the Clover Club is a classic for a reason. Dry gin, grenadine, lemon juice and egg white create a smooth, frothy sip with just the right amount of tartness. Shake it up, strain it into a glass, and enjoy a drink that's as charming as it is refreshing.

Ingredients

- Dry gin
  2 oz. (60 ml/4 tbsp.)
- Splash grenadine
  1 oz. (30 ml/2 tbsp.)
- Lemon juice
  1 oz. (30 ml/2 tbsp.)
- Egg white

Method

Shake the ingredients, then strain into a cocktail glass and serve.

COLONEL SOUR

When it comes to sour cocktails, the Colonel Sour knows how to stand out. Bourbon, lemon juice and a touch of sugar create a drink that's both bold and balanced, with a flavour that's sure to command attention. Shake it up, strain it out and let the Colonel take charge of your tastebuds.

Ingredients

- Bourbon
  2 oz. (60 ml/4 tbsp.)
- Lemon juice
  ¾ oz. (22 ml/1 ½ tbsp.)
- Superfine (caster) sugar
  ½ tsp.

Method

Shake the ingredients, then strain into an old-fashioned glass and serve.

SIDECAR

Hop in for a ride with the Sidecar – a cocktail that's smooth, citrusy and just a little bit daring. Brandy, Cointreau and fresh lemon juice create a drink that's perfectly balanced and irresistibly sippable. Shake it up and enjoy the kind of cocktail that turns any night into a special occasion.

Ingredients

- Brandy
  1 oz. (30 ml/2 tbsp.)
- Cointreau
  ⅔ oz. (20 ml /1 ⅓ tbsp.)
- Fresh lemon juice
  ⅔ oz. (20 ml /1 ⅓ tbsp.)

Method

Shake the ingredients, then strain into a cocktail glass and serve.

LIQUEUR

MONTE
STAMBECCO
ITALY
MARASCHINO
CHERRY AMARO

Published in 2025 by Welbeck
An Imprint of HEADLINE PUBLISHING GROUP LIMITED

2

Text copyright © 2025 Headline Publishing Group Limited
Illustrations copyright © 2025 Louise Whittaker

Apart from any use permitted under UK copyright law, this publication may only be reproduced, stored, or transmitted, in any form, or by any means, with prior permission in writing of the publishers or, in the case of reprographic production, in accordance with the terms of licence issued by the Copyright Licensing Agency.

Cataloguing in Publication Data is available from the British Library

ISBN 9781035423446

Printed in China

Headline's policy is to use papers that are natural, renewable and recyclable products and made from wood grown in well-managed forests and other controlled sources. The logging and manufacturing processes are expected to conform to the environmental regulations of the country of origin.

HEADLINE PUBLISHING GROUP LIMITED
An Hachette UK Company
Carmelite House
50 Victoria Embankment
London EC4Y 0DZ

www.headline.co.uk
www.hachette.co.uk

The authorized representative in the EEA is Hachette Ireland, 8 Castlecourt Centre, Dublin 15, D15 XTP3, Ireland (email: info@hbgi.ie)